HOPSCOTCH
EDUCATIONAL PUBLISHING

Starting with...
Role play

Into space

Diana Bentley

Maggie Hutchings

Dee Reid

Diana Bentley is an educational consultant for primary literacy and has written extensively for both teachers and children. She worked for many years in the Centre for the Teaching of Reading at Reading University and then became a Senior Lecturer in Primary English at Oxford Brookes University. Throughout her professional life she has continued to work in schools and teach children aged from 5 to 11 years.

Maggie Hutchings has considerable experience teaching KS1 and Early Years. She is a Leading Teacher for literacy in The Foundation Stage and is a Foundation Stage and Art coordinator. Maggie is passionate about the importance of learning through play and that learning should be an exciting and fun experience for young children. Her school's art work has been exhibited in The National Gallery, London.

Dee Reid is a former teacher who has been an independent consultant in primary literacy for over 20 years in many local authorities. She is consultant to 'Catch Up' – a special needs literacy intervention programme used in over 4,000 schools in the UK. She is Series Consultant to 'Storyworlds' (Heinemann) and her recent publications include 'Think About It' (Nelson Thornes) and Literacy World (Heinemann).

Other titles in the series:

Colour and light
Under the ground
Emergency 999
At the hospital
Fairytales
At the garage/At the airport
All creatures great and small
On the farm
Water
Ourselves
At the shops

Other Foundation titles:

Starting with stories and poems:

Self esteem
Self care
A sense of community
Making relationships
Behaviour and self control

A collection of stories and poems

Starting with our bodies and movement

Starting with sounds and letters

The authors would like to thank Jane Whitwell for all her hard work in compiling the resources and poems for the series.

Published by
Hopscotch Educational Publishing Ltd, Unit 2, The Old Brushworks, 56 Pickwick Road, Corsham, Wiltshire, SN13 9BX
Tel: 01249 701701

© 2006 Hopscotch Educational Publishing

Written by Diana Bentley, Maggie Hutchings and Dee Reid
Series design by Blade Communications
Cover illustration by Sami Sweeten
Illustrated by Debbie Clark
Printed by Colorman (Ireland) Ltd

ISBN 1 905390 14 9

Diana Bentley, Maggie Hutchings and Dee Reid hereby assert their moral right to be identified as the authors of this work in accordance with the Copyright, Designs and Patents Act, 1988.

The authors and publisher would like to thank Chapter One (a specialist children's bookshop) in Wokingham for all their help and support. Email: chapteronebookshop@yahoo.co.uk

Contents

Acknowledgements

The authors and publisher gratefully acknowledge permission to reproduce copyright material in this book.

'Journey into Space' by Irene Yates. © Irene Yates. Reproduced by kind permission of the author.

'Immediate Dispatch' by Jean Gilbert. © 1979 Jean Gilbert. Reproduced by permission of Oxford University Press.

'Playtime' by Penelope Browning. © Penelope Browning. Reproduced by permission of Oxford University Press.

'The Solar System' by Clare Bevan. © Clare Bevan. Reproduced by kind permission of the author.

'Footprints on the Moon' by Marian Swinger. © Marian Swinger. Reproduced by kind permission of the author.

Every effort has been made to trace the owners of copyright of material in this book and the publisher apologises for any inadvertent omissions. Any persons claiming copyright for any material should contact the publisher who will be happy to pay the permission fees agreed between them and who will amend the information in this book on any subsequent reprint.

Introduction

There are 12 books in the series *Starting with role play* offering a complete curriculum for the Early Years.

Ourselves	*At the garage/At the airport*
Into space	*Emergency 999*
At the shops	*All creatures great and small*
Colour and light	*Under the ground*
At the hospital	*Fairytales*
On the farm	*Water*

While each topic is presented as a six-week unit of work, it can easily be adapted to run for fewer weeks if necessary. The themes have been carefully selected to appeal to boys and girls and to a range of cultural groups.

 Each unit addresses all six areas of learning outlined in the *Curriculum Guidance for the Foundation Stage* and the specific Early Learning Goal is identified for each activity and indicated by this symbol.

Generally, differentiation is achieved by outcome, although for some of the Communication, Language and Literacy strands and Mathematical Development strands, extension activities are suggested for older or more confident learners.

Suggested teaching sequence for each unit

Each week has been organised into a suggested teaching sequence. However, each activity in an area of learning links to other activities and there will be overlap as groups engage with the tasks.

The Core Curriculum: Literacy and Mathematics

Every school will have its own programmes for literacy and mathematics and it is not intended that the activities in the units in this book should replace these. Rather, the activities suggested aim to support any programme, to help to consolidate the learning and to demonstrate how the learning can be used in practical situations.

The importance of role play

'Children try out their most recent learning, skills and competences when they play. They seem to celebrate what they know.'

Tina Bruce (2001) Learning Through Play: Babies, Toddlers and the Foundation Years. London: Hodder & Stoughton.

Early Years practitioners are aware of the importance of play as a vehicle for learning. When this play is carefully structured and managed then the learning opportunities are greatly increased. Adult participation can be the catalyst for children's imaginations and creativity.

Six weeks allows for a role play area to be created, developed and expanded and is the optimum time for inspiring children and holding their interest. It is important not to be too prescriptive in the role play area. Teachers should allow for children's ideas and interests to evolve and allow time for the children to explore and absorb information. Sometimes, the children will take the topic off at a tangent or go into much greater depth than expected or even imagined.

Organising the classroom

The role play area could be created by partitioning off a corner of the classroom with ceiling drapes, an old-style clothes-horse, chairs, boxes, large-scale construction blocks (for example, 'Quadro') or even an open-fronted beach tent/shelter. Alternatively, the whole classroom could be dedicated to the role play theme.

Involving parents and carers

Encourage the children to talk about the topic and what they are learning with their parents or carers at home. With adult help and supervision, they can explore the internet and search for pictures in magazines and books. This enriches the learning taking place in the classroom.

Outside activities

The outdoor classroom should be an extension of the indoor classroom and it should support and enhance the activities offered inside. Boys, in particular, often feel less restricted in outdoor play. They may use language more purposefully and may even engage more willingly in reading and writing activities. In the outdoor area things can be done on a much bigger, bolder and noisier scale and this may connect with boys' preferred learning styles.

Observation in Salford schools and settings noted that boys access books much more readily when there is a book area outdoors.

Resources

Role play areas can be more convincing reconstructions when they are stocked with authentic items. Car boot sales, jumble sales and charity shops are good sources of artefacts. It is a good idea to inform parents and carers of topics well in advance so they can be looking out for objects and materials that will enhance the role play area.

Reading

Every week there should be a range of opportunities for children to participate in reading experiences. These should include:

Shared reading

The practitioner should read aloud to the children from Big Books, modelling the reading process; for example, demonstrating that print is read from left to right. Shared reading also enables the practitioner to draw attention to high frequency words, the spelling patterns of different words and punctuation. Where appropriate, the practitioner should cover words and ask the children to guess which word would make sense in the context. This could also link with phonic work where the children could predict the word based on seeing the initial phoneme. Multiple readings of the same text enable them to become familiar with story language and tune in to the way written language is organised into sentences.

Independent reading

As children become more confident with the written word they should be encouraged to recognise high frequency words. Practitioners should draw attention to these words during shared reading and shared writing. Children should have the opportunity to read these words in context and to play word matching and word recognition games. Encourage the children to use their ability to hear the sounds at various points in words and to use their knowledge of those phonemes to decode simple words.

Writing

Shared writing

Writing opportunities should include teacher demonstration, teacher scribing, copy writing and independent writing. (Suggestions for incorporating shared writing are given each week.)

Emergent writing

The role play area should provide ample opportunities for children to write purposefully, linking their writing with the task in hand. These meaningful writing opportunities help children to understand more about the writing process and to seek to communicate in writing. Children's emergent writing should occur alongside their increasing awareness of the 'correct' form of spellings. In the example below, the child is beginning to have an understanding of letter shapes as well as the need to write from left to right.

Assessment

When children are actively engaged in the role play area this offers ample opportunities for practitioners to undertake observational assessments. By participating in the role play area the practitioner can take time to talk in role to the children about their work and assess their performance. The assessment grid on page 35 enables practitioners to record progress through the appropriate Stepping Stone or Early Learning Goal.

DfES publications

The following publications will be useful:

Progression in Phonics (DfES 0178/2000)
Developing Early Writing (DfES 0055/2001)
Playing with Sounds (DfES 0280/2004)

Into space	Role play area	Personal, Social and Emotional Development	Communication, Language and Literacy	Knowledge and Understanding of the World	Mathematical Development	Creative Development	Physical Development
Week 1	Building the space station	*Show a range of feelings* Discussing space and anxieties about the dark	*Hear and say initial sounds* Phonemes 'r' 's' 'm' 'l' Writing labels and discussing space	*Ask questions about how things happen* Discussing astronauts and space	*Count up to 10* Counting up and down to 10	*Use imagination in art and design* Creating spaceship, astronauts, Moon and stars	*Move with control and coordination* Cutting out Starting and stopping
Week 2	Making junk models and astronaut equipment	*Take turns/share* Role playing taking turns and negotiating roles	*Extend vocabulary* Listening and responding to story Using 'space' vocabulary Writing in logbooks	*Build and construct* Building space station Exploring why astronauts use dried foods	*Locate 3-D shapes* Using vocabulary for different shapes Weighing and measuring foods	*Use imagination in art and design* Making breathing tanks and junk models of spacecraft	*Show awareness of space* Moving like astronauts Using modelling tools for making objects
Week 3	Making a collage of the planets	*Understand codes of behaviour* Playing landing on a planet – reduce numbers of children left in game	*Write labels and captions* Revisiting initial sounds Writing labels and captions for planets Reading poems and songs	*Find out about the natural world* Finding out about the planets	*Use language to describe size, shape and position* Sequencing circles according to size Using Roamer for instructions	*Explore colour, shape, texture* Making collage of planets Transforming Roamer into space buggy	*Use a range of equipment* Using scissors for cutting out Playing hoop games and activities
Week 4	Creating the lunar landscape	*Be confident to try new activities* Performing rhymes and poems to others	*Listen and respond to stories* Sharing non-fiction and fiction books and discussing them Making simple books	*Ask questions about how things work* Exploring aspects of the Moon Understanding how craters are formed	*Use maths to solve practical problems* Devising instructions for Roamer Looking at numbers 1–5	*Use imagination in art and design* Creating lunar landscape	*Move with confidence* Miming walking on the Moon Playing star game
Week 5	Making, and marking places on, Earth	*Develop awareness of own needs, views and feelings* Learning and discussing 'Five Little Men'	*Enjoy spoken and written language* Discussing favourite places on Earth Writing list of rules to keep planet beautiful	*Observe and find out about the natural world* Discussion about looking after planet Earth	*Use vocabulary of subtraction* Subtracting numbers from 5 Number matching 1–9	*Use imagination in art and design* Making circle to represent Earth Marking main areas Painting a picture of favourite place on Earth	*Move with control* Playing space game – running to different commands
Week 6	Journey into space and return to Earth	*Respond to significant experiences* Reflecting on the topic and discussing what they enjoyed and learned	*Interact with others, negotiate plans* Going on final journey into space and interviewing each other about adventures	*Find out about objects that have been observed* Exploring the globe and how Earth appears from space	*Use language to describe shape and size* Revisiting 3D shapes and identifying them	*Explore colour, texture, form and shape* Making mobiles of day and night	*Move with confidence and imagination* Following instructions for travelling in space Making further space models from Lego

Into space

In this six-week unit the children will be introduced to the concept of space. Talk, play and activities will revolve around astronauts, space travel, the planets and Earth. Ensure the children all have adequate opportunity to explore the role play area, both with and without an adult. They should use an 'Into Space' dressing-up box (see Resources).

At the end of the unit, as well as contributing to the role play area, the children will have:
• made life-size astronauts
• created a day/night mobile
• made junk models of spacecraft and moon buggies
• created a collage picture showing the relative distance between the planets and the Sun
• created pictures of favourite places on Earth.

WEEK 1

Starting the role play area

This week the role play area is going to become a space station. Start the role play area by covering two wall areas (preferably a corner) with either large sheets of paper or sheeting. This will form the backdrop for the space scene. Make a **large circular window frame** (approximately 90cm in diameter) out of card. Stick this onto the backdrop to be the spaceship window. The children will cut out **silver** or **white stars** and a **Moon**. These should be placed on the backdrop to be seen through the spaceship window. They will also make **life-size astronauts** to display in the role play area (and around the classroom). They will build a **control panel** from cardboard boxes. Place a table and chairs near the window to be the base for the control panel and seats for the astronauts.

Resources

Photocopiables:

Rocket template (page 27)

Fiction books:

Can't You Sleep, Little Bear? by Martin Waddell, Walker Books
(0 744572 94 0)
Rocket Countdown by Nick Sharratt, Walker Books
(0 744578 02 7)

Non-fiction books:

Star Science – Group Discussion Book, Ginn (0 602267 34 X)
Space Equipment, 'Space explorers' series, Heinemann Library
(0 431113 48 3)

Music and song:

'Moon Walking' and 'Dance from a Distant Planet', from *Let's go Zudie-o* (Songs and CD), A&C Black (0 713654 89 9)
'Spaceship to the Moon' from *Bobby Shaftoe Clap Your Hands*, A&C Black (0 713635 56 8)
Space music, such as 'The Planets' by Gustav Holst and 'Thus Spake Zarathustra' by Richard Strauss used in the film '2001: A Space Odyssey'
Bend and Stretch with the Sticky Kids (CD, Sticky Music, PO Box 176, Glasgow G11 5YJ)

ICT and audio-visual:

Colour Magic CD-Rom game, Research Machines
A video recording of a rocket launch or mini video clips from the internet

Website:

www.jsc.nasa.gov

Materials:

- Sticky labels or blank badges
- Lametta (to decorate comet trails)
- Old CDs
- Coloured card (yellow, silver)
- Coloured paper (black and white)
- Large cardboard boxes
- Playground chalks
- Coloured revolving disco light (available from many electrical stores)
- Paints

Dressing-up box:

Begin to resource the dressing-up box with suitable costumes, such as spacesuits made from old silver anoraks and jackets, old dungarees, over-sized gloves, plastic helmets covered in silver foil, Wellington boots (painted silver) and inflatable silver backpacks. (If possible, make simple 'all-in-one' suits with Velcro fastening using silver fabric.) Include toy walkie-talkies.

Knowledge and Understanding of the World

 Ask questions about how things happen and why things work.

Introducing the topic

☐ Brainstorm with the children their knowledge of space and space travel. Ask them the following questions: Where is space? How do people travel in space? What are the people who travel in rockets called? What happens when a rocket is launched?

☐ Show the video clip of a rocket launch.

☐ Discuss with the class what the inside of a spaceship might look like. Think about things such as the controls, computers, consoles, seating, wires and tubes.

☐ Show the children pictures of astronauts from books, magazines or downloaded from websites (such as www.jsc.nasa.gov). Discuss with them what the astronauts are wearing. Ask questions such as: Why do they need to wear a spacesuit? Why do they wear a special helmet?

Personal, Social and Emotional Development

 Respond to significant experiences showing a range of feelings.

Circle time

☐ Tell the children to imagine they are astronauts. Discuss how an astronaut might feel (excitement/ fear). Ask: How would you be feeling before, during and after the launch? Imagine that all is dark outside your rocket as you fly through space – what do you think you would feel?

☐ Make the link between travel into space and times when they have been in the dark. Ask: Do you sleep with a light on? Do things seem different in the dark?

☐ Read *Can't You Sleep, Little Bear?* or another suitable story and invite the children to talk about things that might worry them in the dark. Encourage them to express their own feelings and emotions.

Creative Development

 Use their imagination in art and design.

Creating a space backdrop

- ❏ Cut a large crescent moon shape out of yellow card. Help the children to cut out star shapes from silver or white paper or use strings of silver stars from shops. Create comets with lametta trails. Stick them all onto the circular window in the role play area.

Building the inside of the rocket

- ❏ Cover large boxes with white or black paper and decorate them to create control panels, computers and consoles. (Add numbers, letters and coloured bottle tops and old CDs.)
- ❏ Let the children role play being astronauts and talk about what they see through the spaceship window.

Making 'life-size' astronauts

- ❏ Help the children to draw round each other on large sheets of paper. They should cut out their own body shape and then paint it white, silver or black and decorate it to create an astronaut. Decorate the astronauts with small boxes, plastic lids, plastic food containers or old CDs.

- ❏ Display the astronauts around the classroom in various positions – for example, suspended from the ceiling or in the role play area.

ICT

- ❏ Use a painting program, such as *Colour Magic* (see Resources), to create rocket shapes. Demonstrate how to select tools and use the mouse. Ask the children to create their own designs. Print the designs and display them in the classroom.

Music

- ❏ Play some 'space' music (see Resources). Ask the children to imagine they are flying through space in a rocket. You could use a coloured revolving disco light to create a dramatic effect. (Check that none of the children is affected by strobe lighting before doing this.)

Mathematical Development

 Count reliably up to 10.

Counting up and down to 10

- ❏ Share with the children a pop-up book such as *Rocket Countdown* (see Resources).
- ❏ Ask them to count to 10, using their fingers. Then count back from 10 to 0 (as for a rocket lift-off).
- ❏ Give the children copies of the rocket template (page 27). This time, as they count to 10, tell them to place a block (such as a Unifix cube) in each of the squares on the rocket. When they have covered all the squares on the rocket, ask them how many blocks there are. As they count back to 0, they can take blocks away.

Outside activities

- ❏ Draw a large rocket template with 10 squares in chalk on the playground. Ask the children to count with you up to 10. As you count, ask a child to place a building block into each square. Ask them how many blocks there are. As you count back to 0, invite individual children to take a block away.

Extension

- ❏ Laminate a rocket template with missing numbers up to 20 to make a 'Write on – wipe off' activity. Ask the children to fill in the missing numbers.

Building the space station

Communication, Language and Literacy

 Hear and say initial sounds in words.

Phonics

❑ Introduce initial phonemes, such as 's' for 'Sun', 'space station' and 'star', 'r' for 'rocket', 'm' for 'Moon' and 'l' for 'launch'. Use familiar words and ask the children to listen for the initial sound and then identify the phoneme. Encourage them to suggest other words and to identify the initial phoneme. Play 'I spy' with words linked to the theme, such as 'a' for 'astronaut'.

Writing labels

❑ Make labels for the role play area. Scribe for the children words such as 'computer', 'stars', 'control panel' and 'deep space'. Ask for suggestions from the class. Encourage them to supply the initial phoneme and demonstrate the grapheme that represents that phoneme.

❑ Make labels or badges for the children to wear to gain entry into the space station – Captain, Crew 1, Crew 2, Mechanic, Engineer.

❑ Make a second set of labels for the children to find and match.

Vocabulary extension

❑ Share *Star Science – Group Discussion Book* (or similar) about space (see Resources). Introduce the key language of space and encourage children to use this in role play.

Shared writing – teacher modelling

❑ Label one of the 'life-size' astronauts created in Creative Development with words such as 'helmet', 'spacesuit', 'gloves' and 'boots'.

❑ Tell the children you are going to write a sentence on the board about the astronauts – for example, 'Astronauts wear special clothes.' As you write it talk through the writing process, explaining capital letters, spaces between words, phonemes and so on.

Outside activities

❑ Write the initial phonemes 's', 'r', 'm' and 'l' on the playground with chalk. The children have to jump on the phoneme as either the sound, or a word with that initial letter, is called out.

Physical Development

 Move with control and coordination.

Practising fine motor skills

❑ Cutting out stars for the backdrop to the role play area and astronaut shapes (see Creative Development).

❑ Manipulating small objects – putting Unifix blocks onto rocket template (see Mathematical Development).

❑ Hand–eye coordination – using the mouse to create a rocket (see 'Colour Magic' CD-Rom in Resources).

Movement and gymnastics

❑ Instruct the children to start (countdown from 10, crouching on floor) and to blast off (arms in air and stand up). Tell them to move quickly across the floor and then, on instruction, to slow down and stop (land). Tell the children to check they are in their own space.

❑ Play the song 'Zooming to the Moon' from *Bend and Stretch with the Sticky Kids* (see Resources) and encourage the children to move around like spacemen.

❑ Dance to 'Moon Walking' and/or 'Dance from a Distant Planet' from *Let's go Zudie-o* (see Resources) or other space music.

WEEK 2

The role play area

During this week the children will be making 3-D junk models of spacecraft, rockets, space stations, flying saucers and **space buggies** to add to the role play area.

The teacher or adult helper will make **breathing tanks** from plastic bottles and plastic tubing for moon walking and **logbooks** for the children to record their travels. The children will role play going to and landing on the Moon.

Play atmospheric music and sound effects, such as a rocket launch, to enhance the children's role play.

breathing tanks

log books

space buggy

Resources

Photocopiable:

Poems and songs 1 (page 28)

Fiction books:

Happy birthday, Moon by Frank Asch, Aladdin Picturebooks (0 689835 44 2)
Meg on the Moon by Helen Nicoll, Puffin (0 140501 20 7)

Non-fiction books:

Roaring Rockets by Tony Mitton, Kingfisher (0 753403 61 X)
Rockets and Spaceships by Karen Wallace, 'Dorling Kindersley Readers' (0 751329 10 X)
Space Travel, 'Space Explorers' series, Heinemann Library (0 431113 45 9)
Living in Space, 'Space Explorers' series, Heinemann Library (0 431113 47 5)

Poetry:

Poems About Space compiled by Brian Moses, Hodder Wayland (0 750224 40 1)

Music and song:

Recording of 'Spaceman Sid' (www.earlybirdsmusic.com)

ICT and audiovisual:

A video clip of a rocket launch

Materials:

- Construction kits, bricks and 3-D shapes
- Balloon
- Drinking straw
- Fine string or fishing line
- Bulldog clip
- Packets of dried foods, such as dried milk and soup
- Scales
- Logbooks (exercise books covered in silver paper)
- Materials for space vehicles – garden canes, masking tape, tinfoil, paper for flags, dowelling
- Cubes, cuboids, cylinders and cones
- Playground chalks
- Simple modelling tools

Visiting space

Personal, Social and Emotional Development

 Take turns and share fairly.

Taking turns

- ❑ Provide plenty of opportunities for the children to take turns in the role play area and in the classroom. Talk to them about why we take turns. Involve and support them in turn taking activities – for example, 'John has been the commander of our ship. Now it's Amy's turn,' and 'Sarah has played the game on the computer. Can Joe have a turn now, please?'

- ❑ Help them to get in role by using the character badges (from week 1) and by setting up scenarios in the spaceship, such as take-off or landing. Encourage the children to negotiate, to listen to each other and to respond. Explain that they should play in the spaceship cooperatively and show sensitivity towards others.

- ❑ Explicitly praise children who share willingly – for example, 'I noticed how nicely James waited for his turn.'

Knowledge and Understanding of the World

 Build and construct.

Building space equipment

- ❑ Provide a range of construction kits, bricks and 3-D shapes and encourage the children to build a rocket or space station. Can they select appropriate shapes to balance? Can they join construction pieces together? Can they adapt their work where necessary?

How a rocket works

- ❑ Show the video clip of a rocket launch. Talk about how a rocket works (by propulsion). Its engines burn fuel which makes a very hot gas. When the gas is forced out, it pushes the rocket along. Inflate a balloon. Let it go. It flies because of the force of the air leaving it, much like a rocket.

Making a simple rocket

- ❑ Thread a short length of straw onto a piece of fine string or fishing line. Tie the string or line between two chairs, ensuring it is taut. Inflate a long balloon and fasten the neck with a bulldog clip to stop it deflating. Attach the balloon to the straw using masking tape. Place the balloon and straw at one end of the line. Release the bulldog clip and watch the balloon-powered straw travel like a rocket! Talk about what is making the straw move.

Reading about space

- ❑ Share with the children an information book about space (see Resources). Introduce specific vocabulary as you look at the pictures, such as 'planet', 'satellite', 'shuttle', 'space station' and 'space buggy'. Encourage the children to talk about where their rocket might land.

Life and work in space

- ❑ Talk about life and work in space – the difficulty of weightlessness and floating. Explain that astronauts' food is vacuum-packed or they have dried food, because fresh food would go off.

- ❑ Show the children a selection of dried foods. Let them handle the food and smell it in its dried form. Then add hot water and talk about the changes in consistency and appearance.

Creative Development

 Use their imagination in art and design.

Making junk models

- ❑ Make junk models of the following – spacecraft, rockets, space stations, flying saucers and buggies.

☐ Make breathing tanks for on the Moon. Use two large plastic bottles taped together and attached with elastic shoulder straps. Use small lengths of plastic tubing to represent oxygen supply lines.

Outside activity

☐ Create a moon buggy using tricycles or other stable vehicles. Working with small groups of children, give them the opportunity to work cooperatively and to convert them into lunar or fantasy space vehicles. Let them experiment, explore and create – for example, attach garden canes or lengths of dowelling with flags to the vehicles. Use masking tape and tinfoil to cover the frame. Weave silver strips of foil between the spokes.

Communication, Language and Literacy

 Extend vocabulary.

Speaking and listening

☐ Read *Happy birthday, Moon* or a similar story about the Moon (see Resources).

☐ Encourage the children to talk about their model making. Use adult talk to guide them into modifying actions – for example, 'That piece didn't look right. What else could we use? We could try a flatter shape but I'm not sure if it will be big enough.'

☐ Encourage the children to use objects to represent things – for example, 'We need a nose on the rocket. Which shaped brick could we use?'

☐ Listen to the song 'Spaceman Sid' (see Resources). Help the children to identify some of the rhyming words – for example, 'Sid' and 'Blid', 'far' and 'star'.

☐ Read a selection of poems and songs from page 28.

Drama

☐ Participate in role play – for example, 'This is the spacecraft to take me to the Moon. Will you come with me? Let's put on our spacesuits.' (Pretend to get ready while the children put on costumes and breathing tanks from the costume box.) Ask the children what it feels like to wear a spacesuit.

Hot seating

☐ Ask for a volunteer to sit in the hot seat. Explain that it is the captain's chair (or a crew member's seat) in the spaceship. Give the volunteer the captain's helmet to wear. Create a simple scenario, such as 'The spaceship is setting off to explore a planet far away in the galaxy.' Ask questions such as: What happened when you…? What did you wear? What did you eat? How did you feel when … happened? When you landed on the planet, did you see anyone? Were they friendly?

Shared writing – teacher modelling

☐ Discuss with the children a sentence you could write about the food astronauts eat, such as 'Astronauts take dried food into space because it is very light.' Talk through the writing process, explaining capital letters, spaces between words, phonemes and so on.

Writing – teacher scribing

☐ Scribe suggested menus for the astronauts.

Extension

☐ More able children could illustrate and label their own menu.

Independent writing

☐ Make two or three logbooks for the role play area. Write the title 'Captain's Log' on them. Encourage the children to experiment with emergent writing, to draw pictures or to write some simple sentences each time they visit the role play area.

Outside activity

☐ Use chalk to write some letter shapes on the playground. Play games where you say a word and children have to jump on the letter shape that matches the initial phoneme of the word.

Visiting space

Mathematical Development

 Locate 3-D shapes.

Using shapes

- ❏ Collect a variety of different shaped objects – cylinders, cubes and cuboids. Investigate these shapes in relation to rockets and other space vehicles – for example, a rocket is a cylinder with a nose or cone at the top and a moon buggy is a cube or cuboid with wheels.

Measuring

- ❏ Add a cone to different sized cylinders to make rockets. Use these to compare height/length.

Weighing

- ❏ Using scales, compare the weight of some dried food, such as packet soup, before and after water has been added.

Extension

- ❏ Ask the children to pick up different shapes as you call them out. Ask them how many sides the shape has, how many corners and how it rolls.
- ❏ Ask the children to predict whether the dried food or the reconstituted food will be heavier. Why is this?

Physical Development

 Show awareness of space, of themselves and of others.

Movement

- ❏ Tell the children that they are all astronauts. Say that there is very little space in the rocket at the launch so they must stand as close as they can to you, without touching you or anyone else. Imagine the rocket has landed on the Moon. Now the children can explore the Moon by walking and keeping as far away from everyone (and the sides of the room) as they can.
- ❏ Vary this by suggesting running, tiptoeing, striding or standing close to a named child.
- ❏ Tell the children that they are to climb into the rocket so they have to walk up ten steps. Then they should lie down close to one another but not touching, ready for take-off. When they arrive they have to take ten steps down out of the rocket onto the Moon's surface. Then they should walk as though they are weightless. They should explore the Moon's surface by taking big steps but keeping as far away from everyone as they can.

Fine motor control

- ❏ Using modelling dough, encourage the children to explore its malleability by squeezing, prodding, rolling and patting. Introduce and encourage the children to use the vocabulary of manipulation – for example, 'squeeze', 'soft', 'squashy' and 'lumpy'.

Extension

- ❏ Provide some simple modelling tools, such as knives and trowels, and allow time for exploration. Then ask the children to make a specific object – for example, a space rocket. Encourage them to talk through in advance what they plan to make and help them to reflect on what they have done.

WEEK 3

The role play area

This week the children are going to make a large-scale **collage of the planets** to add to the black backdrop. They will be transforming the Roamer into a **space buggy** and making a **class reference book** about the planets.

collage of the planets

class reference book

space buggy (Roamer)

Resources

Photocopiables:

Poems and songs 2 (page 29)
The solar system (page 30)

Phonics: *Progression in Phonics*, National Literacy Strategy, DfES (Ref no. DfES 0178/2000)

Non-fiction books:

Planets Big Book, Heinemann Library (0 431014 68 X)
Astronaut – Living in Space by Kate Hayden, Dorling Kindersley Readers (0 751362 61 1)
The Planets, 'Space Explorers' series, Heinemann Library (0 431113 44 0)
Space, 'EyeWonder' series, Dorling Kindersley (1 405304 73 1)

A selection of posters of the planets

Materials:

Collage material
*   Sun: scrunched tissue paper in red and orange
*   Mercury: shades of lilac (torn paper strips from magazines)
*   Venus: sponge printing with orange and yellow
*   Earth: blue background with green paper shapes of continents
*   Mars: red scrunched tissue paper
*   Jupiter: pastel stripes of pink, orange, yellow and brown
*   Saturn: chalk stripes of yellow, white and orange from top to bottom of planet – rings drawn in same colours circling the planet
*   Uranus: green and white torn strip of tissue paper
*   Neptune: shades of blue pastels (merge colours with fingers)
*   Pluto: white paper
*   Sheets of A3 paper for planets
*   Sheets of A3 black paper

*   A scrapbook
*   Hoops

Visiting the planets

Knowledge and Understanding of the World

 Find out about the natural world.

Introducing our solar system

☐ Help the children to find out about the planets. Look at videos, pictures, posters, and simple reference books of the planets in our solar system. Encourage them to share their findings with others.

☐ Give the children copies of 'The solar system' (page 30). Talk to them about the names of the different planets and their appearance. Tell them to colour the planets appropriately.

Creative Development

 Explore colour, texture, shape and form and develop fine motor skills.

Making a collage of the planets

☐ Make a collage of each planet to show its relative size and its distance from the sun. Cut out nine different sized circles explaining to the children which planet each circle will represent. Ask the children to create each planet (see Resources).

☐ Put the Sun at one edge of the backdrop and discuss with the children where to place each planet.

Shared writing – teacher modelling

☐ Discuss with the children a suitable title for the collage – for example, 'Our solar system'. Then write a caption, such as 'Which planet is nearest to the Sun? Which planet is furthest from the Sun?'

ICT

☐ Transform the Roamer into a space buggy by adding objects such as tubes and boxes.

Physical Development

 Use a range of equipment.

Fine motor control

☐ Ask the children to cut out planet shapes from paper. Let them decorate their planets using torn paper and stick-on paper shapes. Encourage them to experiment with colour by using chalks and then merging the colours with their fingers. They should place their planets on an A3 sheet of black paper.

Movement

☐ Explore circles using hoops. Give each child a hoop. Tell them to walk round their hoop, then to draw the hoop in the air. Next, ask them to draw a circle with their foot, then jump/hop into their hoop, and jump/hop out of their hoop. Then tell them to move across the floor, around all the hoops. On 'Go', they should run and stand in someone else's hoop, then go back and stand in their own hoop.

Communication, Language and Literacy

 Write labels and captions.

Independent writing

☐ Make labels for the planets. Scribe for less confident children or write the the names in highlighter pen for them to write over. More able children could refer to a chart or poster and write their own labels. Stick one set of labels on the planets. Make an extra set of labels for word matching games.

Phonics

☐ Revisit initial sounds, referring to planet names – 'S' for Saturn, 'M' for Mercury and Mars, 'J' for Jupiter, 'P' for Pluto, 'V' for Venus and 'N' for Neptune.

☐ Play 'Circle swap shop' (*Progression in Phonics* Step 2 – see Resources). Work with a small group of children. Give each child an object (or a picture of the object) and tell them to sit in a circle. Call out a phoneme and children with an object which starts with that phoneme must swap places. Ask all the children to repeat the phoneme.

Listening

❏ Read a selection of poems and songs from page 29.

Independent writing – labels

❏ Make a simple book from black sugar paper or use a scrapbook. Give each child a planet to cut out, colour and label. Discuss with them how the planets should be ordered in the book – from biggest to smallest, from hottest to coolest?

❏ Encourage the children to add information to the logbooks in the form of text or pictures.

Extension

❏ More able children could work in pairs to make 'lift-the-flap' labels. On folded paper they should write the name of the planet on the outside and inside they should write a fact about the planet, such as 'very cold', 'has moon' or 'has rings'. Attach the labels to the collage.

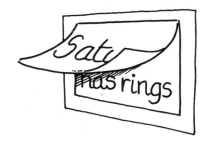

Mathematical Development

 Use language to describe size, shape and position.

Sequencing by size

❏ Make circles of different sizes from thin card. Ask the children to put them in order of size. Start with the smallest, then the largest. (The children could either do this as a tabletop activity or hold up circles for another child to put in order.)

Mathematical language

❏ Introduce vocabulary such as 'near', 'far', 'nearest to', 'furthest away', 'behind' and 'in front'. Play games: Who is the nearest to the door? Who is standing behind…? Who is furthest away from the television? Can you stand in front of the table?

❏ Revisit 3-D shapes. Remind the children that all planets are spheres. Compare them to a globe, balls, beads and so on. Discuss the properties of a sphere (a solid shape with no sharp edges).

Extension

❏ Make a collection of spherical shapes of different sizes. Ask the children to put them in order according to size and to describe their shapes.

ICT

❏ Show the children how to program the Roamer to move forwards a chosen distance; for example, across the circle to another child.

Personal, Social and Emotional Development

 Understand codes of behaviour – accept winning and losing.

Musical hoops

❏ Scatter hoops (one per child) in the playground or hall. Tell the children these are planets in the solar system. When the music stops they must run to a hoop. Ask them to name the planet they have landed on. After several goes, remove two hoops. Those children who do not get to a hoop when the music stops must sit down quietly at the side. Continue until there are approximately six children left. Replace the hoops two by two until all the children are back on their planets.

Into space

WEEK 4

The role play area

This week the children will create a **lunar landscape** and display their **junk models** from Week 2 against this background. They should imagine that a small craft is launched from the space station to land on the Moon. Wearing their moon boots, they will explore the lunar surface. They will program the **Roamer as a space buggy** to transport raisins from one point to another.

lunar landscape

junk models

space buggy (Roamer)

Resources

Photocopiables:

Poems and songs 3 (page 31)
The one-cut book (page 34)

Fiction books:

Any big book of nursery rhymes
Whatever next? by Jill Murphy, Macmillan (0 333636 21 X)
Bring Down the Moon by Jonathan Emmett, Walker Books (0 744589 50 9)

Non-fiction books:

Bubbles Big Book, Cambridge University Press (0 521564 59 X)
The Moon, 'Starters' series, Hodder Wayland (0 750242 83 3)
The Moon, 'Space Explorers' series, Heinemann Library (0 431113 41 6)

Music and songs:

A recording of traditional nursery rhymes

Materials:

- Photographs of the Moon (from books, magazines or the Internet)
- Sheets of black or dark blue sugar paper
- A length of textured white wallpaper
- Ready-mixed white and silver paint
- A small packet of raisins
- A marble
- Plaster of Paris
- Pasta shapes
- Rice

Knowledge and Understanding of the World

 Ask questions about why things happen.

Understanding more about the Moon

❏ Look at photographs and pictures of the Moon. Introduce the idea of phases of the Moon. Read *The Moon* (see Resources). Explain that the Moon has no light; it looks bright to us because it reflects the Sun's rays. The Sun is the only source of natural light in the galaxy. Ask the children to observe the Moon before they go to bed and share their observations with the others. Ask: What shape Moon did you see? What else did you see in the night sky? Did you see patterns of stars?

❏ Talk about travel to the Moon. Ask the children to consider whether people can live on the Moon.

Making a Moon crater

❏ Talk about shapes on the Moon – craters. Explain that craters could have been made by large rocks crashing onto the surface of the Moon. Experiment with making craters by dropping a marble into wet plaster of Paris. Observe the effects.

Shared writing – teacher modelling

❏ Write some sentences to describe what happened when the marble hit the plaster of Paris – for example, 'When we dropped a marble into the plaster of Paris it made a dent. It looked like a crater on the Moon.' Talk through the writing process, explaining capital letters, spaces between words, phonemes and so on.

Extension

❏ The children could refer to books showing the sky at night and identify the patterns of the stars.

Creative Development

 Use imagination in art and design.

Outside activity

❏ Using ready-mixed paint, flick white and silver paint onto dark blue or black background paper. Ask the children to help you to create a lunar landscape using the splatter painted sheets as background and textured white wallpaper for hills and craters (see Physical Development). Display the 3-D models from week 2 in the role play area against this background. Encourage the children to talk about what their vehicles are doing and where they are going.

Mathematical Development

 Using mathematical methods to solve practical problems.

ICT

❏ Remind the children how to program the Roamer to move forwards. Ask them to show you how this is done. Then demonstrate how to make it move backwards.

❏ Give two instructions: move 3 forward and 3 back. Link this to a storyline from the unit – for example, 'Roamer is a space buggy taking food to a space station.' The children should work with a partner and sit opposite each other. One child programs the Roamer to deliver something to his or her partner – a small item of food, such as a raisin, in a small container attached to the back of the robot. Allow plenty of time for the children to explore, practise and make mistakes.

Concept of number

❏ Draw simple star shapes all over a whiteboard. Choose a number from 1 to 5 and ask the children in turn to circle a group of stars of that number.

The lunar landscape

Extension

- ❑ Do the same star activity but choose a number from 6 to 10.
- ❑ Cover a piece of A4 card with PVA glue. Scatter rice or very small pasta shapes onto the card. When dry, write a number, for example, 7, at the top of the card and ask the child to ring groups of seven.

Outside activity

- ❑ Play the star game. Tell the children they are each little stars. The stars are going to join together to make a big star like the Sun. When you call out a number they must form clusters or groups of that number as quickly as they can. When they are in their star cluster they should count to check they are the right number.

Physical Development

 Move with confidence, imagination and in safety.

Fine motor control

- ❑ Cutting skills – white wallpaper hills and creative for lunar landscape (see Creative Development).

Moving with control and coordination

- ❑ Star game – moving with control and coordination (see Mathematical Development).
- ❑ Tell the children to mime putting on moon boots. Then they must move around slowly with heavy feet. Then they should take off their moon boots and run around with light, quick footsteps.

Personal, Social and Emotional Development

 Be confident to try new activities.

Drama

- ❑ Support less confident children to take lead roles in role play.

Rhymes and songs

- ❑ Sing nursery rhymes, such as 'Twinkle, Twinkle, Little Star' and 'Hey Diddle Diddle'.
- ❑ Read 'Footprints on the Moon' from page 32. Encourage the children to join in. Invite groups of children to perform the poem for the others.

Communication, Language and Literacy

 Listen with enjoyment and respond to stories, songs and other music.

Listening

- ❑ Read stories about the Moon and share non-fiction books with the class (see Resources).

Phonics

- ❑ Say the nursery rhyme 'Hey Diddle Diddle'. Talk about the rhyme. Discuss rhyming words and look at the shape of words and rhyming sounds in print. Do the same with 'Twinkle, Twinkle, Little Star'.
- ❑ Play rhyming couplets (see page 31). Ask the children to supply the rhyming word at the end of the line.
- ❑ Play 'Granny went to market'. Help the children to think of items in alphabetical order – for example, astronauts, boots, camera, dried food and so on.

Shared writing – teacher scribing

- ❑ Discuss with the children what they would take to the Moon. Scribe some of the suggestions.
- ❑ Help the children to make simple books (the one-cut book – see page 34). They could draw pictures of the Moon on each page showing the different phases or draw some different planets.

Independent writing

- ❑ Encourage the children to add further information to the logbooks in the role play area.

Extension

- ❑ More able children could add labels or captions to each page of their book.

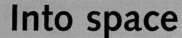

WEEK 5

...ds **planet Earth** to study it from space. They will see the
la... ...o look after the planet.

planet Earth

spaceship

land

ocean

Resources

Photocopiables: ... ...'A Family Concert' MCA

Poems and songs 4 (...

Phonics: *Progression in* ...
DfES (Ref no. DfES 0178/...

Fiction books:

Five Little Men by Mal Peet, Collins Educational (0 003012 33 6)
Why should I protect nature? Worldwide Fund for Nature,
Hodder Wayland (0 750236 83 3)
What if? 'Wonderwise' series, Franklin Watts (0 431113 42 4)

Non-fiction books:

Rockets and Spaceships by Karen Wallace, 'Readers' series,
Dorling Kindersley (0 751329 10 X)
The Earth, 'Space explorers' series, Heinemann Library
(0 431113 42 4)

- ..., green, brown
- A range of paintbrushes
- A globe
- Hoops

Into space

The role play area

This week the children go on an imaginary journey, starting off with a rocket journey into space. They will set off in the early morning and visit the Moon and the planets. They can add to the logbooks and then return to planet Earth in the evening when it is getting dark. They will make **day and night mobiles** to remind them of the different things we see in daylight and at night.

Resources

Photocopiable:

Lacing cards (page 33)

Phonics: *Progression in Phonics*, National Literacy Strategy DfES (Ref no. DfES 0178/2000)

Fictions books:

And the Good Brown Earth by Kathy Henderson, Walker Books (0 744581 41 9)
Daisy and the Moon by Jane Summers, Orchard Books (1 841218 98 7)

Non-fiction book:

Night and Day, 'Reading About' series, Franklin Watts (0 749648 33 3)

Materials:

- A globe
- Hoops
- Black or dark blue paper and yellow or pale blue paper

Creative Development

 Explore colour, texture, shape, form and space.

Making mobiles

❑ Create mobiles representing day and night. Wrap strips of black or dark blue paper around half the hoop for night and light blue or yellow strips of paper for the day. Encourage the children to select their own materials and to make, paint or draw things related to day or night, such as the Sun, clouds, flowers and animals; the Moon, stars, an owl and a fox. Ask them how they plan to make their mobile and what they will need. Attach their work to the hoops and suspend them from the ceiling. Encourage them to talk about their work. Ask: Did it turn out as you hoped? Do you need to add anything else? Do you want to change anything?

Communication, Language and Literacy

 Interact with others, negotiate plans and activities and take turns.

Reading

❏ Fill the role play area with books and reference materials used in this topic and encourage the children to browse, talk to each other and share information. Adults should encourage the children to use the vocabulary used over the last five weeks.

Phonics

❏ Play 'Noisy letters' (*Progression in Phonics:* Step 2 – see Resources). Choose five different letters. Give each child a card and tell them to hide it behind their back. They walk around the classroom, making the sound of the phoneme on their card and group together with other children making the same sound. Then they should check that everyone in the group has the card with the same grapheme.

Songs and poems

❏ Revisit songs and poems explored during the unit.

Vocabulary extension

❏ Take groups of children on final journeys into space and back to Earth. Encourage them to read and make final entries in the logbooks (started in Week 2). Some children may want to write simple sentences, such as 'I was the commander of the spaceship.' Be prepared to be their scribe.

❏ Encourage the children to interview each other about their exploits in space. Tell them to choose a badge to identify their role and to dress up if they like. Other children should ask them questions, such as 'What could you see from your spaceship?' and 'Was it bumpy when you landed on the Moon?' Take a role yourself, either as a crew member or as an interviewer.

Knowledge and Understanding of the World

 Find out about objects that have been observed.

Exploring the globe

❏ Discuss the different countries of the world. Look at the globe. Ask: Which countries are hot? Which countries are by the sea? Do you know people who live in other countries?

❏ Show the children some Internet pictures of the Earth from space. What can they identify (sea, land, rivers)?

Mathematical Development

 Use language to describe the shape and size of solids and flat shapes.

Revisit 3-D shapes

❏ Challenge the children to identify a sphere, a cube, a cuboid or a cylinder. Show them a picture of a rocket and ask which 3-D shapes they can identify.

❏ Ask the children some questions – for example, hold up a cube and ask 'Why isn't this shape a triangle?' (Because it doesn't have three sides.) Look down a cylinder. What shape can you see at the end?

The final journey

Guess the shape

- ❏ Put a selection of 3-D shapes into a feely bag. Invite the children to describe what they can feel – for example, 'This shape has four straight sides,' and 'This shape is curved.'

Estimate

- ❏ Ask the children to sit in a big circle. Challenge them to estimate the distance across the circle and program the Roamer to travel to a particular child. Did it travel far enough? What must ~~~~ time to be m~~~~

Extension

- ❏ Ask the grou~~~~ needed to tra~~~~

Phy~~~~

Move wi~~~~ in safety.~~~~

The space game

- ❏ Play the space ga~~~~ Reinforce the rule~~~~ ~~~~ instruction for travelling – for example, 'reverse'.

Fine motor control

- ❏ Provide an opportunity for the children to create more space models using construction resources.

- ❏ Stick enlarged copies of page 33 onto thick card to make some simple lacing cards of rockets and stars. Help the children to thread and undo.

Personal, Social and Emotional Development

Respond to significant experiences.

Looking back

- ❏ ~~~~se this week to reflect on the topic. What do the ~~~~ildren remember? What are they most proud of?

~~~~d writing – scribing/supported composition

- ~~~~cuss with the children which aspect of the topic ~~~~y enjoyed most. Tell them they are going to write ~~~~tences about their favourite thing. Orally ~~~~arse these sentences with them, such as 'Amy ~~~~d making the Moon craters.' and 'Joshua liked ~~~~ing the moon buggy.' Some children may like ~~~~rite their own sentence independently. Others ~~~~ write over your highlighter writing or you ~~~~ write the sentence for them. Give them the ~~~~tunity to write their sentences on the ~~~~uter using a concept keyboard if appropriate.

- ~~~~d the poem 'Five Little Men in a Flying Saucer' (page 32). Ask: Why do you think the five little men were disappointed with what they saw on Earth?

Review and evaluation

Encourage the children to reflect on the topic. What have they enjoyed learning about? Which part has been most exciting? Which stories and songs do they remember? Which artwork did they most enjoy doing? Would they like to travel through space?

Journey into Space

We went on a journey
A journey, a journey.
We went in a rocket
Jaswinder and me.

We went past the Moon
And we went past the planets.
We sailed into Sunspace
Jaswinder and me.

We landed at daybreak,
At daybreak, at daybreak.
We landed in secret,
Jaswinder and me.

Then the aliens found us
And danced all around us.
And made plans to crown us
Jaswinder and me.

But we climbed in our rocket,
Our rocket, our rocket,
And zoomed back to earth
Just in time for tea.

Irene Yates

We're off to the Moon

(Sung to the tune of 'Bobby Shaftoe')

Climb aboard the silver spaceship (x3)
We're off to the Moon.

Start the countdown, fire the rockets (x3)
We're off to the Moon.

Slowly lift off from the launch pad (x3)
We're off to the Moon.

Zoom, zoom, zoom to outer space (x3)
We're off to the Moon.

Dee Reid

Immediate Dispatch

Polish up the spaceship,
Shine, shine, shine,
Fill up the fuel tanks
In time, time, time,
Switch on the motor
And close down the hatch.
Moonship Apollo
Immediate dispatch.

Shooting into outer space
Zoom, zoom, zoom,
Circling round and round the earth
There's room, room, room,
Watch every lever
And check every clock.
Moonship Apollo
Is ready to dock.

Jean Gilbert

Rocket rhyme

10, 9, 8, 7, 6, 5, 4
Here is a rocket
ready to roar.

3, 2, 1
Blast off to the sky
There goes the rocket.
Wave bye-bye.

Tony Mitton

Countdown

See the shiny rocket
Standing on the launch pad
See the happy astronauts
One, two, three.
Turn on the engine
Fasten all the seat belts
Let's start the countdown
Count with me.
10, 9, 8, 7, 6, 5, 4, 3, 2, 1
LIFT OFF

Dee Reid

Playtime

Let's fly to the Moon to play today
In spacesuits the colour of lead,
On moonbeams we'll ride, in our spaceship
  we'll hide,
But I want to come home to my bed.

Let's shoot to the stars to play today,
We'll go in a rocket instead,
We'll sparkle today and shine while we play
And then I'll come home to my bed.

Let's go on a rainbow to play today
'Midst yellow and orange and red,
We'll have lots of fun and play in the sun,
But I want to come home to my bed.

Penelope Browning

My telescope

I bought myself a telescope
To look into the sky,
To see the solar system
And the comets whizzing by.

I search the sky for planets,
For satellites and stars,
And now I've got a telescope
They don't seem very far.

It's brought them very close to me
It's made the stars my friends –
Except, of course, when I make a mistake
And look through the wrong end!

Tony Bradman

Star Light, Star Bright

Star light, star bright,
First star I see tonight,
I wish I may, I wish I might,
Have the wish I wish tonight.

Anon

Twinkle, twinkle

Twinkle, twinkle little star
How I wonder what you are
Up above the world so high
Like a diamond in the sky
Twinkle, twinkle little star
How I wonder what you are.

Anon

The Solar System

Magical Mercury zooms
Through the night,
Venomous Venus is
Misty and bright.

Earth is the place where
We curl up in bed,
Mars is a planet
That's dusty and red.

Jupiter still has a spot
On its face,
Saturn wears rings as
It sparkles in space.

Uranus floats like a
Gassy balloon,
Neptune's as blue as a
Dreamy lagoon.

Pluto is tiny and turns
Far away –
That's all the planets.
There's no more to say.

Clare Bevan

The solar system

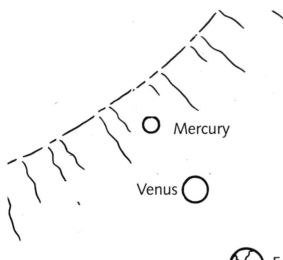

Mercury

Venus

Earth

Moon

Mars

Jupiter

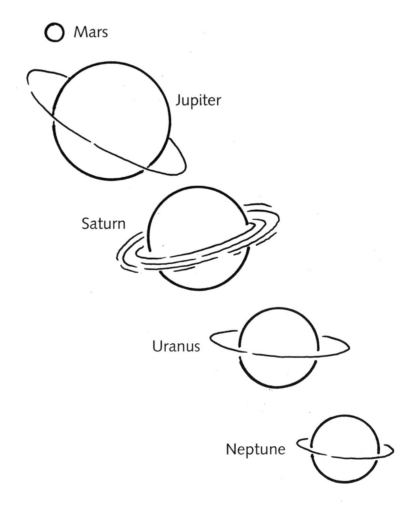

Saturn

Uranus

Neptune

Pluto

Rhyming couplets

At night I wonder why
Stars twinkle in the _____ (sky)

Travel far
To see a _____ (star)

Late at night
Turn off the ____ (light)

Man in the Moon
I'll see you ____ (soon)

The planet Mars
Is near the ____ (stars)

Take a trip
In a space ____ (ship)

3, 2, 1
Off to the ____ (Sun)

Have a race
Into _____ (space)

The Moon shines bright
In the sky at _____ (night)

Come on, get on board

(Sung to the tune of 'Here we go round the Mulberry Bush')

Matthew has a big spaceship, a big spaceship,
a big spaceship
Matthew has a big spaceship
So come on, get on board.

Amina is in the big spaceship, the big
spaceship, the big spaceship
Amina is in the big spaceship
She's going to the Moon.

Continue adding other children's names.

Dee Reid and Diana Bentley

Visiting the Planets

(Sung to the tune of 'Coming round the mountain')

We are rockets zooming round in outer space
    (zoom, zoom) (2)
We are rockets zooming round
Rockets zooming round
Rockets zooming round in outer space
    (zoom, zoom)

We are off to explore the planet Mars
    (red dust) (2)
We are off to explore
Off to explore
Off to explore the planet Mars (red dust)

We are whizzing off to visit Jupiter (sixteen
    moons) (2)
We are whizzing off to visit
Whizzing off to visit
Whizzing off to visit Jupiter (sixteen moons)

Saturn is the planet we'll see next (lots of
    rings) (2)
Saturn is the planet
The very big planet
Saturn is the planet we'll see next (lots of
    rings)

Dee Reid

Poems and songs 4

Our beautiful world

Look around
What do you see?
Fields and hedges
Hills and a tree.
It's a beautiful world
For you and me.

Look around
What do you see?
Sandy beaches
Waves on the sea.
It's a beautiful world
For you and me.

Look around
What do you see?
Flowers in a garden
One, two, three.
It's a beautiful world
For you and me.

Dee Reid

Footprints on the Moon

There were men on the Moon once.
They travelled through space
Found that the Moon
Was a dry, dusty place.

They collected some Moon rocks
And had a look round
And left lots of footprints
There on the ground.

They couldn't stay long
As the Moon had no air,
But the footprints they left
In the dust are still there.

Marian Swinger

Five Little Men in a Flying Saucer

Five little men in a flying saucer,
Flew round the world one day,
They looked left and right,
But they didn't like the sight,
So, one man flew away.

Four little men in a flying saucer,
(etc)

Three little men in a flying saucer,
(etc)

Two little men in a flying saucer,
(etc)

One little man in a flying saucer,
Flew round the world one day,
He looked left and right,
But he didn't like the sight,
So, then he flew away.

Anon

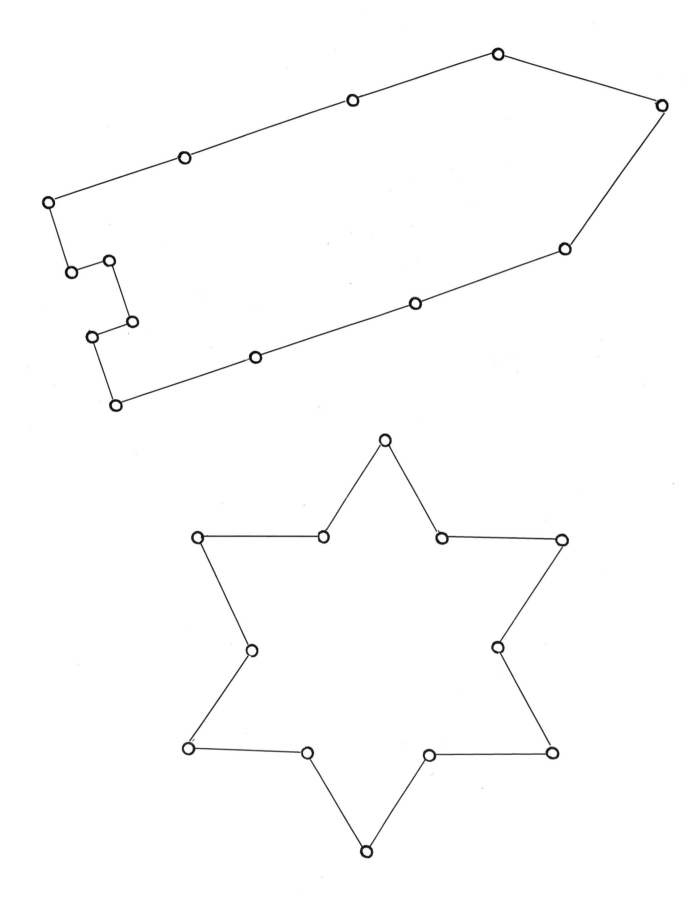

Photocopiable

One cut book

You will need:

❑ a piece of A3 paper

❑ scissors

What to do:

❑ Fold the paper in half lengthways, then in half widthways, then in half again widthways to form eight rectangles. (Figure 1)

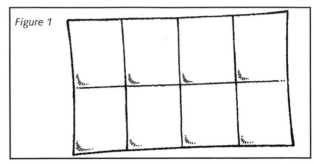
Figure 1

❑ Open the paper and fold widthways, making a sharp crease. (Figure 2)

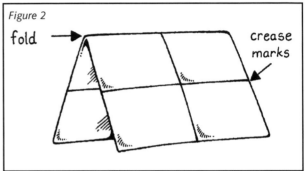
Figure 2
fold → crease marks

❑ Cut from the folded edge to the 'cross' of the creases. (Figure 3)

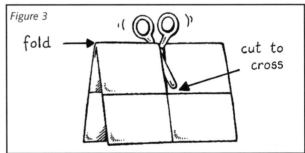
Figure 3
fold → cut to cross

❑ Open the paper completely and fold lengthways. Push left and right ends into the centre. (Figure 4)

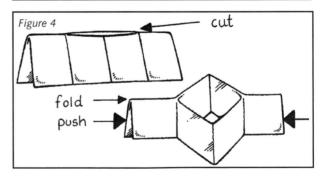
Figure 4
cut
fold → push →

❑ Fold round to form front and back of book. (Figure 5)

Figure 5
crease firmly

Unit: _____   Class: _____   Date: _____

Name	Personal, Social and Emotional Development	Communication, Language and Literacy	Knowledge & Under-standing of the World	Mathematical Development	Creative Development	Physical Development
	Y B G ELG	Y B G ELG	Y B G ELG	Y B G ELG	Y B G ELG	Y B G ELG
	Y B G ELG	Y B G ELG	Y B G ELG	Y B G ELG	Y B G ELG	Y B G ELG
	Y B G ELG	Y B G ELG	Y B G ELG	Y B G ELG	Y B G ELG	Y B G ELG
	Y B G ELG	Y B G ELG	Y B G ELG	Y B G ELG	Y B G ELG	Y B G ELG
	Y B G ELG	Y B G ELG	Y B G ELG	Y B G ELG	Y B G ELG	Y B G ELG
	Y B G ELG	Y B G ELG	Y B G ELG	Y B G ELG	Y B G ELG	Y B G ELG
	Y B G ELG	Y B G ELG	Y B G ELG	Y B G ELG	Y B G ELG	Y B G ELG
	Y B G ELG	Y B G ELG	Y B G ELG	Y B G ELG	Y B G ELG	Y B G ELG
	Y B G ELG	Y B G ELG	Y B G ELG	Y B G ELG	Y B G ELG	Y B G ELG
	Y B G ELG	Y B G ELG	Y B G ELG	Y B G ELG	Y B G ELG	Y B G ELG
	Y B G ELG	Y B G ELG	Y B G ELG	Y B G ELG	Y B G ELG	Y B G ELG
	Y B G ELG	Y B G ELG	Y B G ELG	Y B G ELG	Y B G ELG	Y B G ELG
	Y B G ELG	Y B G ELG	Y B G ELG	Y B G ELG	Y B G ELG	Y B G ELG
	Y B G ELG	Y B G ELG	Y B G ELG	Y B G ELG	Y B G ELG	Y B G ELG

Circle the relevant Stepping Stones (Y = Yellow; B = Blue; G = Green or ELG = Early Learning Goal) and write a positive comment as evidence of achievement.